by all means . . .

JUST SAY IT

"A collection of thought provoking poetry…
that speaks to the silence that needs to be heard"

LORI BEST YEAGER

B.E.S.T.™

(Be the **E**nd to **S**ilent **T**houghts)

**Healing begins when the Silence Ends;
No one battles alone**

www.thehopeforbest.com

Library of Congress Control Number: 2021916815

Yeager, Best Lori
 by all means. . .JUST SAY IT

Tradepaper ISBN: 978-0-578-97121-6

Printed in the United States of America

◆

To you . . .

reading this book . . .

May you find inspiration,

peace, comfort

and healing.

◆

CONTENTS

◆

Introduction vii

◆ UNFORESEEN LOSS ◆

Always Three 2

Hear Your Cry 3

Unaswered Whys 4

Never Ready 5

Mournful Day 6

Tattooed Heart 7

Picture 8

Estranged 9

◆ UNEASY TURMOIL ◆

You May Not Know 11

Battles 12

Urge 13

Change 14

Captivity 15

Habits 16

Addiction 17

Tangled Web 18

◆ BE YOU ◆

Connection 20

Blank Slate 21

What's Inside 22

Under Pressure 23

Words 24

Stand Up..25

Spark 26

Unique..27

Fitting In..28

Pretend 29

Blending...30

Race..31

Story...32

Position 33

Shoe...34

Assume..35

◆ ENLIGHTEN MY PATH ◆

Seasons..37

Thrive..38

Feather...39

Rainbow 40

Today...41

Set Free 42

Happiness 43

Beauty 44

Mistakes 45

Defeat 46

Choice 47

Million Pieces 48

Measured Love..49

◆ MOVED BY FAITH ◆

Overcome...51

Pain Too Deep 52

Eyes Awake 53

Awaken..54

Everywhere 55

Pride...56

Umbrella Prayer..57

Feed 58

Snake 59

Shadow..60

Angel 61

Real Faith..62

Final Note 63

Acknowledgements..65

INTRODUCTION

On November 1, 2018, my life changed. Not ever did I think this could happen to us! As cliché as it sounds, "we had no idea, we truly were blindsided." This day, moved me in a direction that I never thought I would be traveling. The road ahead, filled with many emotions and unanswered "whys," paralyzed me. Numb at first, the first few weeks were just a blur. Sleep filled most of my days and evenings because to be "awake" meant I had to think about it. However, slowly I came to the realization that it did not matter how much I slept or how much I stayed awake. My current situation remained the same. I must travel this road, whether I want to or not.

To this day, and unfortunately probably forever, I will never get over the sadness. It was awful. It just takes hold and hangs onto your every being. You wish, just wish for one day for it to go away, but it remains. So, I decided that I had a choice to make: let it control me or I control it? I chose the latter.

On November 1, 2018, at approximately 5:25 a.m. my triplet brother, 49 years old, was taken by suicide. A vibrant, fun, intelligent, full of life, brother, son, uncle, father, husband, friend, colleague, Dan Best, lost the battle that none of us even knew existed. As silent as his thoughts were, they must have been louder than life in his head. A daily cover-up of smiles and laughs—and his were so contagious— kept his pain and hopelessness hidden and silent from everyone. What a terrifying battle to face alone. WHY? Why are so many of us (ALL of us because NOT one person is free from stress, anxiety, sadness...some type of mental struggle) silently battling? Is it fear of failure, judgement, pride? Seems silly when we ALL have a battle that we face.

After Dan's death, I became more aware of my surroundings and people. I constantly looked to nature and/or people to see if I could find any glimpse of Dan; not in the physical sense, but spiritually to connect and know that he was okay. On November 5, 2018, I was blessed to receive this connection!

I was on my way home from the bookstore. I was picking up a copy of *Jesus Calling*, by Sarah Young, for my brother's wife, Lisa. She was coming into town to prepare for the funeral arrangements. It was a dark, ugly day. As I was driving on the highway, I noticed a bright light in the sky. I did not think much of it, so I kept driving. However, there was this nagging feeling to really take a good look at the light. Finally, I succumbed to the urge and pulled over on the highway. I took a picture and went home. Once developed, the photo revealed to me that Dan is absolutely OK. He is with God. The images in the photo were comfortably overwhelming.

At first, I was afraid to talk about his death, stigma, of course. But slowly, I realized this is the PROBLEM! Gradually, I opened up and began telling people that my triplet brother, only two minutes older than me and less than 40 days from our 50th birthday, died. Death by suicide NOT committed suicide— because suicide was a mental state that took his life. I was amazed by people's reactions. Some were family, some friends and others were just acquaintances. They engaged me, no judgment, and shared their own stories of struggles and suffering. I could not believe how many of us shared similar stories and all it took was not to be afraid to talk about it. The door was now open. I knew I had to do something.

I honestly believe it was overcoming this barrier that led me to where I am today. About three months after Dan's passing, I could not sleep. I was constantly woken by thoughts, words and ideas that filled my head. They were so persistent. I tried to ignore them and go back to sleep. It never worked. They just kept coming, keeping me awake. So, I decided to befriend them. I stayed awake. I cannot explain it, but I know God and Dan were all behind it. They were keeping me awake, making sure I wrote it all down. It amazed me the peace that would follow. Well, for many nights and days, I wrote and wrote and wrote. What a blessing for it became the birth of "The Hope for B.E.S.T" (**B**e the **E**nd to **S**ilent **T**houghts).

The umbrella, which encompasses all mental health, knows no bias. It does not matter your race, gender, age, religion, or social status. NO ONE IS IMMUNE. My sealed bag of "silent thoughts" may be different than yours, but we are both holding a bag. "The Hope for B.E.S.T." has one purpose: to STOP the SILENCE so we can open up and start healing. It is OK if you are not OK, for neither am I, or your neighbor, friend, spouse, co-worker.... The battle is no longer "yours" it's "ours." So, let us walk together and **B**e the **E**nd to **S**ilent **T**houghts!

DAN BEST

Photo taken 11 5 18

UNFORESEEN
LOSS

◆

ALWAYS THREE

Three, we will always be

Triple the blessing they received,
when we were conceived

Snuggled in one womb of love,
created by the touch of God's love

A miracle that cannot be denied,
as we were born side-by-side

A connection so unique,
it makes us complete

Some may not understand,
but we just go hand in hand

So, no matter where "you" are,
it is never too far

"Your" presence will always be felt

We will always be together...

Three, we will always be,
Tim, Dan, and me

HEAR YOUR CRY

"I hear your every cry, as I see you struggle
with not knowing the why"

" Please know there was nothing you could have done,
my weary head was just ready to be with the Son"

"I'm sorry that I had to go, I know you didn't know
one day you will understand, oh His amazing grace
welcomed me with open hands"

"My spirit will always be with you,
let me show you how this is true" ....

Hear that little bird singing across the way,
that's me whispering it's all going to be okay

Those colors of the rainbow that you see above,
are signs of my everlasting love

That random penny you found on the street,
I am the one who placed it at your feet

Remember the dream you had about me last night,
it's just me letting you know you are never out of my sight

"I'm sorry that I had to go, I know you didn't know
one day you will understand, oh His amazing grace
welcomed me with open hands"

"My spirit will always be with you,
let me show you how this is true" ....

UNANSWERED WHYS

Take those unanswered "whys"
and toss them to the sky

Don't carry their weight or it will be checkmate;

They will capture you,
falsely giving you thoughts
and ideas that may not be true

Thus, weighing you down,
stealing your hope,
and leaving you letdown

Instead, give them to Him,
for He knows the pain you're in...

He will guard your heart,
protecting you from falling apart

One day the "why" will be known
for He placed it as His thrown

There it will stay, until it is time to be given away

NEVER READY

Never ready or prepared are we,
when God calls our loved ones up to be

Heaven's gate opens wide,
for Angel's wings to carry them inside

Here they will rest, getting ready for God's request

For soon they will have their wings too,
and forever watch over you

MOURNFUL DAY

It is your life that I will remember,
not that mournful day in November

For these memories allow me to see you again,
bringing you back, every now and then

And one day, I will see the light,
and our souls will come together,
in an everlasting life

TATTOOED HEART

It is the weeks, months and years that follow,
that like to keep me captive in death's sorrow

Forever tattooed on my heart
the realization, we are now apart

Memories hold me up for a while,
Oh I am so thankful for their ability to make me smile

The pain that remains, seems to never go away,
but I have learned I can't let it permanently stay

For eventually, peace comes through,
with the ability to help me through

PICTURE

Your picture hangs on my wall,
shared memories capture it all

So full of life and fun were you,
people longed to be around you

Your contagious smile, always followed by a laugh,
I can see and hear it in this photograph

Constantly making time to enjoy the simple things,
to so many, this meant everything

You never knew a stranger, you embraced everyone,
as if they were someone

Your love was real, a simple drop anyone could feel

Your short time here will be sorely missed,
if I could just blow you one more kiss

The picture on my wall, says it all

You made the best of your life lived
and gave all that you could give

Your memory will always live on
and that helps me remain strong

ESTRANGED

My circumstances may have changed,
but I am still the same

Please take this to heart,
when you're not sure where to start

This is all new to me too, I am just as scared as you

So, embrace me the same way,
before we got the news that day

I have not changed, please don't become estranged

UNEASY
TURMOIL

◆

You May Not Know

You may not know, what I am going through,
as I lie here with a mind so consumed...

All I know, are the words to the voice inside my head,
why can't I make them got to bed?

You may not know, that my laugh hides all the crying,
while my smile is hopelessly lying...

All I know,
I am fighting to get out of this zone,
It seems its all I've ever known

You may not know,
I have been walking this road for a while,
carrying the pain with every mile...

All I know, this journey is getting longer,
Oh Lord, I pray I get a little stronger

You may not know,
that I am praying for some peace tonight,
fearing there is no end in sight...

All I know, tomorrow will be another day,
please Lord, don't let me be its prey

BATTLES

If I could make it go away,
I would have done it yesterday

Battles that I face, seem to know their place

Showing up just in time,
falsely claiming a victimless crime

Pulling me in with lies,
ones they hope I don't recognize

The reality of my day is real,
a battle I constantly feel

URGE

The urge to give in, lies somewhere within

It likes to tempt you everyday,
with its very persuasive cunning way

Enticing as it may seem,
it ends in regret by all means

Ironic as it is...

The voice that convinced you to give in,
is the same one convicting you of your sin

CHANGE

Sometimes, change is what we need,
so why are we so hesitant to proceed?

Are we too comfortable with where we are,
making us afraid to venture too far?

Is it the path of the "unknown"
that might keep us from a milestone?

Either way, remember this...

Even the smallest of change can shed some light,
possibly providing us with new insight

CAPTIVITY

Some of the best times in our lives
are when we are free,
so why do we revert back to captivity?

Is it the false hope in our addictions,
that bring us back to our conviction?

Is it the lies we tell ourself,
in order to prevent us from getting help?

Whether captive or free,
they both require a commitment to be

Will you continue to live in deception,
or break free from destruction?

HABITS

Bad habits can often begin,
from buried struggles within

Left untouched, bad habits can become our crutch

Appearing harmless at first,
falsely satisfying feelings submersed

Numbing the pain for a while,
only to return more hostile

Your struggle is still there,
and now you have more to bare

Your impulse to return to them,
allows the battle to never end

Bring those suppressed feelings to the surface,
so your bad habits have no purpose

ADDICTION

It is true, addiction is cruel

It doesn't matter what it is:

Sex, drugs, food, alcohol...
too many to name them all

A sweet taste at first, hidden with a curse

Once you give in, the struggles begin

Unwanted behaviors arrive,
encouraging you to enjoy the ride

You pray for control, as you witness its toll;

Harming you and your loved ones too

NEVER give in to doubt this is
NOT what your life is about

You can turn this chaos around,
and with help your lost self will be found

TANGLED WEB

It is harder to live within your lies,
for their tangled web never dies

Slowly spinning you around with ease,
for is there any harm in what others cannot see?

However, eventually that web will entangle you,
holding you captive with a lot more to do

BE YOU

CONNECTION

Whether we believe it or not,

We are all connected by love and despair,
and when it comes to the pains in life, no one is spared

Instead of gazing at me, with that heavy stare,
and pretending that your own pain isn't there...

Join my circle,
the one that begins with the same end in mind,
that we're all trying to get through life just fine

Often it's when we round
the corner of our own imperfections,
the truth is revealed to us;

That we are all broken in someway
and together we need to make a way;

To stop the silence and talk,

Judgement has no room here; let's all lend an ear

When we refuse to hide behind our own lies,

It's like a breath of fresh air,
we are no longer alone and able to share

When I open up and listen to you,
I find it actually helps me too

So, join my circle,
that connects us all through love and despair,
so we can all know that someone cares

BLANK SLATE

Life is a canvas, you are the artist

Each day a blank slate, what will you create?

Your emotions splatter the surface,
with strokes that seem to have no purpose

However, what you paint today,
may be the colors that had their say;

Blue might show up because of a recent breakup

Red likes to be there in times of despair

Yellow is true and always sees you through

Orange is optimistic
and tends to come when you're more simplistic

More colors may find their way
purple, green, brown and gray

Remember this,
you are the only one who could have painted this

May you find beauty and peace in your masterpiece

Although you may see a mess,
you have no idea who your masterpiece will bless

WHAT'S INSIDE

If all we see is the outside,
we lose the opportunity to know the inside

It's the inside where the truth is revealed,
the outside is often just a shield

So, when judging a "book by its cover",
remember it's the inside you want to discover

Under Pressure

Pressure from others can be brutally strong,
jeopardizing what you know to be right from wrong

Before you join the crowd,
will your behavior make you proud?

If it doesn't feel right to you,
walk away and don't follow through

Your decision to stand up against
what you know to be wrong,
may inspire others to follow along

WORDS

The words you say can make
or break someone's day

Don't disregard their power,
choose to empower

You won't regret it and they won't forget it

STAND UP

Be the smile on his or her sad day,
and speak up against the rumors that "they" say

Alone, that person felt,
until you spoke up against what they were dealt;

Wrongfully characterized,
with an attempt to demoralize

Brave are you and the victim too...

Standing up for what is right,
and defeating "them" in their plight

SPARK

In one moment,
you can be the spark for that person
hiding in the dark

Sad and alone, they thought no one had known

The pain they were going through
because of the cruel words said by just a few

But you knew,

And you chose to speak words of kindness
which helped take away their sadness

As simple as it may seem,
your gesture meant everything

UNIQUE

Hold on to what you know to be true,
and don't listen to the lies they say about you

As a group, they can only exist,
for it's their own insecurities
that cause them to persist

Alone, they can't stand,
for they shamefully understand;

What they are doing to you would hurt them too

So, stand tall and never let their "weakness"
change your "uniqueness"

FITTING IN

By nature, we long to belong...
unfortunately, society has it all wrong;

"Fitting in" begins "within"
NOT with trying to "fit in"

You are the "best" version of yourself,
you are like no one else

Belong to yourself first, then you won't be coerced

To be someone you're not
which can leave you stressed and distraught

You will find that you will be admired
for not doing what others require

PRETEND

You are stronger than them,
you don't have to walk around and pretend

You believe in yourself, and rely on no one else

"They" depend on hurtful lies, trying to get a rise

"Their" confidence doesn't come from within,
only from the "group"
they are trying to "fit in"...

How exhausting it must be,
having others tell you how to be!

BLENDING

I tried to "blend in", just to be their friend

They were the "popular" ones,
according to everyone

It seemed so important at first,
but things got worse

I allowed my true colors to be camouflaged,
to later have them sabotaged

I knew what they were doing was wrong,
but I still went along

Now I am in a jam,
"who's going to believe who I really am?"

I should have listened to myself,
instead of everyone else

RACE

I'm in this race, and feeling out of place

Pretending to be something I am not,
was the wrong thing I sought

Why did I try to keep up with them?
They aren't my friend

Friends don't judge on your "have and have-nots",
and friendships should never be bought

I am no longer out of place,
for I have chosen to leave this race

STORY

We all have a story to tell, I am sure you do as well

If we just took the time to listen, it may alter our position

Understanding another's struggles and success,
leaves no room to guess

Take the time to hear their story,
you may find yourself less discriminatory

POSITION

We can always find something wrong;

If it doesn't match up to what we believe,
we are so quick to leave

Take a moment to listen, regardless of your position

Doesn't mean you have to conform,
just educate yourself on another's platform

SHOE

I wish this world was a better place

Not all of it's bad, but plenty make me sad

One thing I try to do, is put myself in someone else's shoe

Although the shoe may not fit,
it gives me a chance to admit;

We're all broken and need to be more open;

To understanding the challenges other people face,
therefore, hindering any disgrace

This world would be a much better place, no doubt,
if we were willing
to learn what another's life is about

ASSUME

You may want to assume,
but what you don't see is actually how it may be

Before you create your opinion,

The truth should be learned,
in order for you to discern

What "you" may perceive as being true,
may be completely opposite
of what they are really going through....

ENLIGHTEN
MY PATH

◆

Seasons

Seasons can often bring upon change,
offering new perspective in exchange

A colorful fall foliage may lose its leaves,
only to spring back with new life to receive

So, whatever season you are in,
look for new possibilities to begin

THRIVE

There are times in our lives,
when everything seems to thrive

It all just falls into place, "these" are the times to embrace

Too often, when things are going well,
"worry" likes to come in and dwell

Reminding us of fallen days, with conviction,
"this too will end that way"

So, lock the door on any doubt,
for fear loves to push hope out

Enjoy the moment at hand,
removing all of worry's demands

FEATHER

I finally realized that a rip in my feather is actually better

I am still able to fly,
but now with more compassion in my eye

A few scares myself,
lets me recognize the struggle in someone else

RAINBOW

Is there any end in sight,
to generations of differences ending in fights?

Although we disagree,
we should never consider the other a "nobody"

Our lack of similarities, should bring more clarity;

That our world is full of colors,
because of the differences of others

Like a rainbow in the sky,
we should be able to sit side by side

TODAY

We can't change our past, we can hope in our future,
thus, we must live in the now

Yesterday has come and gone,
today will start with a new dawn;

Full of opportunities and choices...

Make no mistake,
there are consequences in the choices you make;

Will they haunt your yesterday,
believing your tomorrow will be just as gray?
OR
Will they be a reminder
that your strength got you through,
giving you hope that tomorrow will too?

The choice is yours, will it be a day of regret?
OR
The beginning of a new mindset?

SET FREE

The weight of our pain,
can hold our forgiveness in chains

Locked deep inside,
it's a burden we carry out of our own pride

However, it's in forgiveness that WE are set free,
lightening our load, so we may finally just BE

HAPPINESS

To love, learn not to judge

To live, learn to forgive

To laugh, learn to give yourself a break,
we all make mistakes

Happiness is a choice, listen for its voice

BEAUTY

Beauty is all around,
it's when you choose to see it, that it's found

Sometimes it's right in front of you,
but you allow your pain to block its view

Just allow a glimpse to come in, you will be amazed
how it removes some of your pain within

MISTAKES

The mistakes of your past,
don't have to "define" you, let them "refine" you

Perfection isn't the aim, it's in growing that you gain

Ignore any negative chatter,
it's your steps forward that matter

DEFEAT

Don't feel defeat, when you've been beat

Competition is good, when you've done the best you could

Win or lose, look at it from a different view;

A chance to learn and grow, then apply what you know

No one is ever a loser, just an improver

Choice

Choice is a decision;

What will you choose?

Good or bad? Happy or sad?

Acceptance or denial? Hope or trials?

At the end of the day,
your choice will be what led you on your way

Million Pieces

When your life seems to be crashing down
into a million little pieces;

Don't worry about trying to pick them
all up at the same time,
inevitably, there will be pieces left behind;

Sometimes, those are the pieces you needed to let go,
and you didn't even know

In time, your pieces will come back together,
maybe not the same as before,
but leaving you new opportunities to explore

MEASURED LOVE

Sometimes words are not enough

Although spoken with beauty, they can fall on ears mutely

Your intent may have been good, but you misunderstood;

It is not always about the words you say ...

It is the attention and time together,

that can be "loves" measure

MOVED
BY FAITH

OVERCOME

I have overcome this pain before
by leaving its anguish outside my door

Refusing to let it back in,
sometimes, takes all my strength within

For around the clock, it continues to knock;

Challenging all the strength I have left,
in pursuit to suppress

It's when I turn back to prayer,
that I am reminded that God is there

My strength, alone,
may not have been able to pull me through,
but with God I am able to

PAIN TOO DEEP

Dear Lord, please hear my heart cry out in prayer,
For my sorrow is so deep and too hard to bear;

My new reality is not what I had planned,
my grieving mind struggles to understand

"Sweet child, I live in you,
and have borne witness to all you have been through"

"Lay your sorrows at My feet,
rest my child, and get some sleep"

The morning dawn will carry My light,
spreading radiant glimpses of new hope in sight"

Eyes Awake

Before the sun arises and our eyes awake,
our dear Lord covers our mistakes

His grace is new every day,
so be sure to thank Him when you pray

Try to walk in step with Him,
you'll be less likely to fall to sin

As the sun goes down and you close your eyes for the night,
don't worry if you didn't get it right

A new grace tomorrow will bring,
a beautiful gift from our King

AWAKEN

Awaken my soul, oh Lord,
for it has been at rest for too long

Beaten by life's burdens,
my soul is weak yet yearns to be strong

"Child, your heart's desire is not by mistake,
your burdens alone, were not for you to take

Your call upon Me has let Me in,
I will awaken thy soul and let strength begin"

EVERYWHERE

You are everywhere, during our trials and in our prayer

You're the vibrant rainbow after the storm,
during labor before a child is born

In the struggle of a butterfly in its cocoon,
during the harsh winter before the flowers bloom

You are everywhere and anywhere

Although my eyes may not see,
my heart knows the blessing that will come to be

PRIDE

It's our pride, that pushes Him aside

We get by for a while, until we are alone in the wild

Roaming the wilderness, feeling its emptiness

It's when we let Him back in, that our life truly begins

He has a plan for you;

Trying to do it alone,
only puts you back in the wilderness to roam

UMBRELLA PRAYER

Dear Lord, please hear my "umbrella prayer"
so many are struggling in pain and despair

My list continues to grow, even for ones I don't even know

Whatever storm they are in,
please watch over and bless them

Give them hope to set them free,
from their raging storms ability

FEED

Be careful what you feed;
it may grow into a weed

First anchoring in your heart,
then spreading to other parts

Choking out any new life,
keeping your hope out of sight

So, you must cut it at the root,
so it may no longer pollute

Only feed the seed you know and believe,
will bear you fruit, sweet and pure,
with only peace to endure

SNAKE

The head
of the snake is
where the poison hides,
just as Satan, the serpent,
tries to fill your head with lies

So, guard your thoughts,
for Satan only has one plot;

To destroy all that is good in you,
which came from God who created you

Therefore, count on your heart to be your guide,
for this is where your goodness resides

SHADOW

In the dark,
a shadow sits, waiting
for light to show it exists

Craving even just a spark,
hoping for the opportunity to unveil its mark

Once shined upon, the shadow looks
back at the light as to say,
"thank you light for coming my way"

"For my image would have never been known,
but for the love that you had shown"

ANGEL

An Angel you truly are, shining brighter than any star

You have always helped me out,
especially when I was down and out

When I thought I was alone,
you included me as one of your one

Never making me feel any less,
when my life was such a mess

A blessing you truly are ...

Thank you for being there for me,
when it seemed no one else could be

REAL FAITH

It is easy to say, but can often be harder to do;

Having faith requires more than just a prayer,

It's your willingness to trust in God's response,
even if it's not what you want

For His plans are always sovereign and of good pleasure,
and ours, alone, would never measure

FINAL NOTE

When traveling on this road called "life," don't worry so much about "where" you are going. Instead, focus more on "who" or "what" you are following. The road, I have been traveling, is not necessarily what I had planned. However, I am thankful that I did not let "where" I was going concern me. Instead, I trusted "who" I was following. For me, God has been my guide. I have followed Him through trials, pain, and disappointments only to have them be shadowed by peace, calm and serenity. I trust Him in my sorrows and blessings. This does not mean my life is any easier; absolutely not. However, it gives me hope, in the road that I am traveling, because I know the good in the One I am following.

Whatever you are going through, trust and know we have all been somewhere on that map. Healing, for me, came through writing and still does. Ironic, because I have never been a writer, ever! I was a criminal justice major, go figure? At the end of the day, if just one of my poems helps someone, I have accomplished something God led me to; First, healing within myself, to then enable me to hopefully help someone else.

The Hope for B.E.S.T. (**B**e the **E**nd to **S**ilent **T**houghts) rose from the deepest depths of my despair. God led me from a tragedy to thoughts, to words, to a voice in order to help others. You can do this too, let's walk together!

Healing begins when the Silence Ends;
No one battles alone

Acknowledgements

This book is the product of the emotions, pain and suffering I experienced after the tragic loss of my brother. His death opened my eyes to mental health issues, not just suicide, but all mental health, the entire umbrella. I spent days, nights and weeks writing as much as I could about it.

I have many people to thank for supporting me on this journey. First and foremost, my amazing husband, Paul. He never left my side. He was my biggest cheerleader! He constantly encouraged me to keep writing and follow what was on my heart. My children, Paul, Jack, Megan, and Michael who always took the time to listen to me recite my poems. My extended "Best Family" and "Yeager Family" who did the same and graciously gave me their time. I am forever thankful!

Family and friends whose photographs are all a part of this book: Tim Best, Colleen Miller, Sue Best Cole, Lisa Best, Kristin Kabelen, Haley Dominique, Mona Koehler, Chris Yeager, Annie Ruprecht, Jill Roach, Carolyn Emerine, Kelsey Flowers, Sue Olson, Amy Hunt, Janet Ruprecht, Megan Yeager, and Erin Turner.

Lastly, there are two amazing people who helped make my dream of writing this book a reality. My dear friend, Laura Tomko, and my sister in law, Bryn Best. Both of them graciously gave their time and talent to editing and laying out this book. I will forever be grateful!

NOTES:

NOTES:

NOTES:

NOTES:

NOTES:

NOTES:

Made in the USA
Middletown, DE
23 September 2022